WHOEVER YOU ARE

WHOEVER YOU ARE

By MEM FOX   Illustrated by LESLIE STAUB

HARCOURT, INC.

Orlando   Austin   New York   San Diego   Toronto   London

Little one,
whoever you are,

wherever you are,

there are little ones
just like you
all over the world.

Their skin may be
different from yours,
and their homes may be
different from yours.

Their schools may be
different from yours,

and their lands may be
different from yours.

Their lives may be
different from yours,

and their words may be
very different from yours.

But inside,
their hearts are
just like yours,

whoever they are,
wherever they are,
all over the world.

Their smiles are like yours,

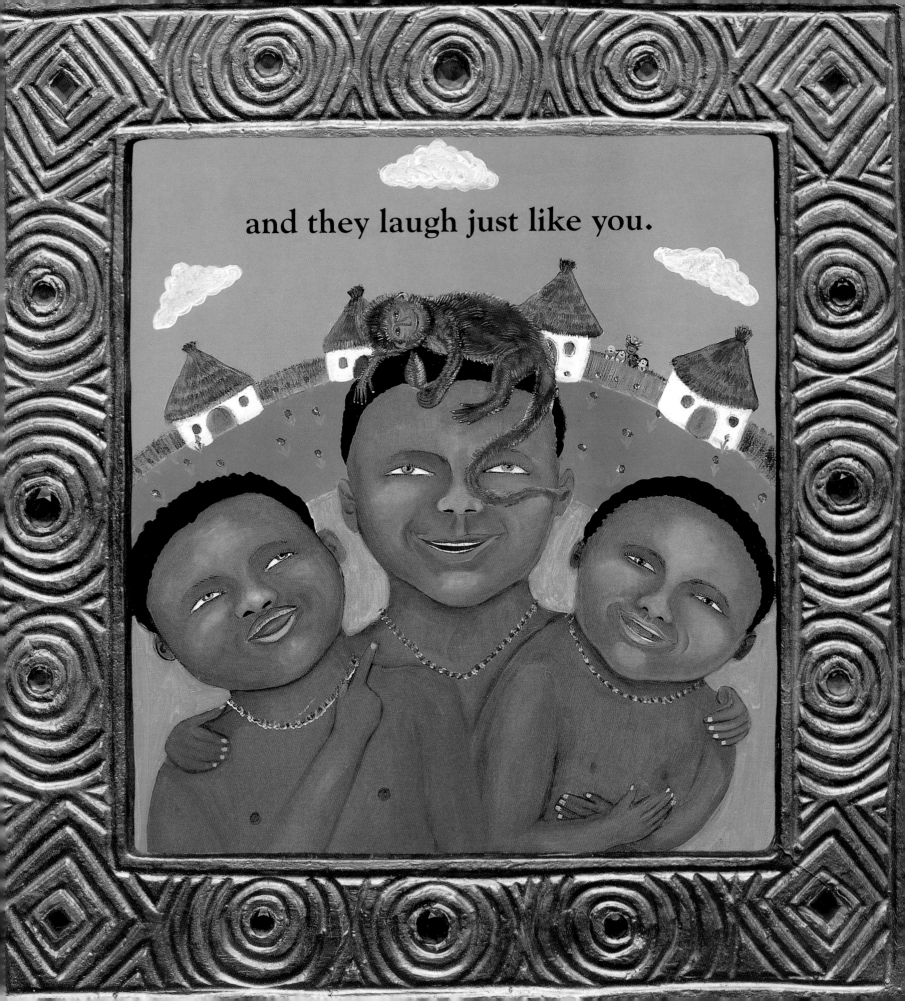

and they laugh just like you.

Their hurts are like yours,
and they cry like you, too,

whoever they are,
wherever they are,
all over the world.

and they may be different,
wherever you are,
wherever they are,
in this big, wide world.

Joys are the same,
and love is the same.

Pain is the same,
and blood is the same.

Smiles are the same,
and hearts are just the same—
wherever they are,
wherever you are,
wherever we are,